The Black Swan

weeded

This book has been reviewed
for accuracy by

Charles M. Weise, Ph.D.
Professor of Zoology
University of Wisconsin—Milwaukee

Library of Congress Number: 78-27416

  2 3 4 5 6 7 8 9 0 83 82 81 80

Printed in the United States of America.

Library of Congress Cataloging in Publication Data

Hogan, Paula Z
   The black swan.

   Cover title: The life cycle of the black swan.
   SUMMARY: Describes the physical characteristics,
habits, and life cycle of the black swan.
   1. Black swan — Juvenile literature. [1. Black swan.
2. Swans] I. Craft, Kinuko. II. Title. III. Title:
The life cycle of the black swan.
QL696.A52H64   598.4'1   78-27416
ISBN 0-8172-1254-X lib. bdg.

The
BLACK SWAN

By Paula Z. Hogan
Illustrations by Kinuko Craft

RAINTREE CHILDRENS BOOKS
Milwaukee • Toronto • Melbourne • London

 # The Black Swan

A flock of black swans fly to a lake. It is winter in Australia and New Zealand. It is time for the swans to breed.

Two swans swim up to each
other. They bow and dip
their heads.

After they mate, the male flaps
his wings. He gives one loud
call. The female calls with him.

The swans make their nest on the water or on land. The male brings grass and sticks. The female builds the nest. Then she lays eggs.

The male black swan watches
the nest in the night. The female
sits on the eggs. When morning
comes, the male sits on the eggs.

Seven weeks go by. The eggs hatch. In about two days, the chicks can swim. Sometimes the mother gives them a ride.

The swans show their chicks
where to find food. They eat
plants growing in the lake. Chicks
must be watched carefully.

Black swans sometimes leave each other after mating. The female cares for her eggs and chicks alone. Sometimes two mother swans help each other.

Slowly the chicks grow gray flying feathers. Chicks cannot fly until they are six months old. Black feathers grow in place of the gray ones as the chick gets older.

The swan has oil on its skin
near the tail. The swan uses its bill
to rub the oil on its feathers. The
oil keeps water off the feathers.

Once each year, grown-up swans lose some of their flying feathers. It takes four months for new ones to grow.

Black swans do not stay with their parents. When chicks are big enough, they leave the nest and their parents.

In summer, the lakes have less water than in winter. The swans fly many miles to marshes near the sea. In winter, the rain comes and fills the lakes. The swans fly back to the lakes to nest.

trumpeter swan

The mute swan is found
in Europe and Asia. It is
often seen in city parks. The
trumpeter swan makes its home in
North America. The black-necked
swan lives in South America.

black-necked swan

mute swan

31

GLOSSARY

These words are explained the way they are used in this book. Words of more than one syllable are in parentheses. The heavy type shows which syllable is stressed.

bill—the hard mouthpart of a swan

black-necked swan—a white swan with a black neck

breed—to mate and raise chicks

chick—a baby swan

flock—a group of swans

flying feathers (**fly**·ing **feath**·ers)—light growths that a swan needs to fly

hatch—eggs opening to let chicks out

marshes (**marsh**·es)—soft wet areas

mate—to join together with a male so that the female can lay eggs

mute swan—a white swan that does not make loud sounds

oil—a greasy material

trumpeter swan (**trum**·pet·er swan)— a white swan that makes long, loud sounds